Books in The Tuttle Twins series:

*The Tuttle Twins Learn About the Law*
*The Tuttle Twins and the Miraculous Pencil*
*The Tuttle Twins and the Creature from Jekyll Island*
*The Tuttle Twins and the Food Truck Fiasco*
*The Tuttle Twins and the Road to Surfdom*
*The Tuttle Twins and the Golden Rule*
*The Tuttle Twins and the Search for Atlas*
*The Tuttle Twins and their Spectacular Show Business*

Find them all at TuttleTwins.com

ISBN 978-1-943521-19-7

Boyack, Connor, author.
Stanfield, Elijah, illustrator.
The Tuttle Twins and the Search for Atlas / Connor Boyack.

Cover design by Elijah Stanfield
Edited and typeset by Connor Boyack

Printed in the United States

10 9 8 7 6 5 4

To Ayn Rand

for encouraging countless people
to think in provocative ways.

"Look at that!" Emily shouted as she pointed to the big circus tent being unloaded from the train.

"I'm so excited to clown around!" Ethan said. "Literally!" he added, laughing out loud.

The twins had won a contest on the radio, earning them two spots as guest clowns in the traveling circus that would be in town for a few weeks.

"Check out this guy," Mrs. Tuttle told the twins, pointing to a large poster as they walked through the parking lot to their trailer, where the family was going to stay while the circus was in town.

"Atlas the Strong," Ethan read out loud. "Look at all the heavy stuff he can lift!"

"I can do that!" Mr. Tuttle replied, flexing his muscles. "No problem!"

"In your dreams," said Mrs. Tuttle, lovingly poking her husband. "I think Atlas has spent a little more time in the gym than you have."

A clown suddenly drove up to the trailer in his tiny car. "Welcome! The name's Kroogie," he said to the Tuttle family. "These must be the special recruits we've been waiting for. Hop on!"

The group drove between rows of trailers and small tents. They passed some acrobats playing a card game and a clown taking a nap.

"This is unacceptable!" the ringmaster suddenly shouted in the distance. The performers gathered around to see what all the fuss was about.

"After everything I did for him, he just up and left," the ringmaster added, showing them a short note Atlas had left behind. It read, simply, "I quit!"

"I guess there was a limit to how many things you could make him lift at once," one clown said, chuckling to himself.

"Deciding to pay him less certainly didn't help, either," another clown added.

The ringmaster glared at him, clearly upset over Atlas leaving the circus.

"Ah, we don't need Atlas," replied another. "He's not that special anyway. He was only one person—why should he get such special treatment?"

"And he was a nobody when he started... this circus made him who he is," Kroogie said, chiming in. "He shouldn't have been so selfish."

The twins joined the clowns to begin practice, and even though the ringmaster was upset, they had a fun time being silly.

Ethan and Emily learned how to juggle, tumble, and even how to mime. They also learned a few magic tricks such as making a stuffed rabbit appear out of a hat!

Ethan and Emily were excited to be a small part of a big circus, and loved learning new tricks and skills.

That evening, all the performers began to gather for a meeting. Some of them were worried that the circus would struggle without its main attraction.

"Maybe there won't be a circus at all," said a dwarf standing on a large crate. The twins recognized the stuntman as Cannonball from the posters. "Atlas was the star, and now he's gone!"

The ringmaster jumped up on the crate. "That doesn't matter!" he said, "I'm in charge here, and we will make this circus work. The show must go on!"

He continued by announcing some changes, including having a parade in town the following day to spread word about the circus and encourage people to come.

The twins did cartwheels during the parade as they walked alongside the other clowns the next day. They waved as they passed their mom and dad, who were cheering and taking photos.

"Where's Atlas?" shouted a man standing near Mrs. Tuttle. "I want to see Atlas!" Several others mumbled in agreement.

The ringmaster forced a fake smile, poking the lion to get it to move around in its cage to capture the attention of the crowd.

Some of the clowns became discouraged and jealous when they heard people shouting for Atlas.

Finally, the day of their first performance had arrived—but the group wasn't ready yet.

"Hurry up, everybody!" the ringmaster spoke into the megaphone. "We're running out of time!"

The construction crew struggled to secure the large tent poles. Atlas used to help, but now he was gone.

Cannonball asked for help feeding the animals because there was too much for him to do alone—but nobody seemed interested. Atlas was always willing to pitch in until the job got done.

The acrobats struggled to carry their tightrope up the ladders. Without Atlas around to give them a hand, they had to do it alone. It was hard work!

As the stands began filling with people, the twins were excited and nervous. Would tonight be a success or a failure, they wondered?

Lights began flashing and the loud music got the audience cheering as the ringmaster welcomed them to the "most amazing circus in town!"

That was the cue for the clowns to come out. The twins joined their costumed friends in the center ring to perform their magic tricks and juggling acts. They were having a blast!

They had practiced plenty, but Ethan had a thought: being a clown wasn't as hard as they thought it would be. It was actually pretty easy, and a whole lot of fun!

Some of the other acts didn't go as well. The acrobats began their routine, but one of them slipped, falling onto the net below. His muscles had become too tired to hold on after all the heavy lifting he had done.

The animals were irritable because they were hungry, so they were not that obedient and didn't perform all their tricks.

Some in the audience started to leave before the show was even over.

"It's all Atlas's fault! He is so selfish!" the ringmaster said, slamming his fist onto a table after the show.

Many of the clowns looked nervous. "What happened tonight was a fluke," Kroogie said reassuringly. "Tomorrow's show will be just fine."

"Will it?" Cannonball replied. "I'm not so sure. We've been taking for granted the value of Atlas's hard work. His strength is what helps make this circus happen—it's also what sells the most tickets!"

"Nonsense," replied the ringmaster. "We all make this circus work together, and the crowds want to see all of us—not just Atlas. We're all just as important."

The ringmaster and Cannonball both made good arguments. As Ethan and Emily listened, they were having a hard time deciding who was right.

"He is just one person," Kroogie concluded. "This show is much bigger than him. Let's get some sleep... we've got rehearsal in the morning."

20

"What's that?" Emily asked the next morning, pointing to a padded table Kroogie was using.

"Oh, this is a massage table," Kroogie replied. "It used to be just for Atlas, but we convinced the ringmaster to let us get massages since he left."

"Finally, we get the perks we've been wanting!" another clown chimed in. "You can get a massage before tonight's show if you want," he told the twins.

"And the food is fantastic!" remarked another. "With Atlas gone, we get to eat this fancy food the chef used to make only for him."

"Before, only Atlas was pampered," said one more. "Now, we all are!"

Ethan wondered why Atlas had been getting such special treatment.

The clowns clearly liked some of the new perks they were getting—but they didn't seem to work as hard as the others or be concerned that the circus might fail with Atlas gone.

During a break, Ethan and Emily watched the elephant dance to the music of the circus calliope.

"Want to give her a treat?" asked the musician in a heavy accent, handing Ethan some peanuts.

Emily smiled as the elephant's large trunk carefully grabbed the peanuts Ethan held out.

The twins noticed the ringmaster walking out of his tent with the chef and the man who did the massages. It looked like they were leaving—but weren't they needed before the circus began? The clowns seemed angry at the ringmaster.

"Ticket sales are slow," the ringmaster explained. "We have to cut costs and make do with less."

As the group of performers were feeling bad for themselves, Cannonball walked by with his backpack on.

"Where are you off to?" the ringmaster asked. "The show starts in two hours!"

"Not for me," he said. "I'm going to search for Atlas."

The twins really liked Cannonball and were sad to see him leave.

"Why do you want to find Atlas?" Ethan asked.

"If this circus has any chance of being successful again, we need him back," Cannonball replied. "And these clowns need to understand that some skills are more valuable than others. No offense to you kids, but being a clown isn't nearly as difficult as being a strongman. Atlas has talent that is harder to replace—and that's why he's more valuable."

"The folks here never really valued Atlas's special skills," Cannonball added. "Sure, he got massages and special meals and more money, but what the clowns don't understand is that he *earned* them."

With that, Cannonball left, leaving one less person to keep the circus going.

Ethan and Emily were concerned with what was happening. Their fun experience was suddenly full of drama, and they wondered which side was right—the clowns and the ringmaster, or Atlas and Cannonball?

"Don't mind him," Kroogie told the twins. "The circus doesn't need him anyway... we've got you!"

"I don't know about that," Emily replied. "If people keep leaving, pretty soon there won't be a circus."

After that evening's performance, the twins told their parents everything that had happened.

"It sounds like the circus is consuming more than it produces," Mr. Tuttle replied.

The twins were confused. "What do you mean?" Ethan asked.

"Well, you *produce* when you make something, and you *consume* when you use it up," Mr. Tuttle said.

"The circus produces something that others want to consume—in this case, entertainment," he added. "Less is being produced without Atlas, so fewer people pay to 'consume' it."

"The clowns also want to consume Atlas's perks," Mrs. Tuttle chimed in. "But they can't produce enough by themselves in order to pay for them."

# PRODUCTION & CONSUMPTION

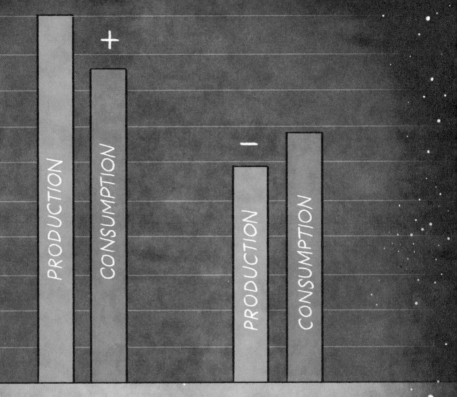

+

PRODUCTION

CONSUMPTION

−

PRODUCTION

CONSUMPTION

WITH ATLAS      WITHOUT ATLAS

GUESTS

By the time rehearsal started the following morning, the twins had made up their mind. "We can't join you today," Emily announced to the group. "We're going to search for Atlas."

Kroogie's jaw dropped, and the ringmaster let out a sigh. "Not again..." he quietly said to himself.

"But you're one of us!" Kroogie said. The painted smile didn't hide his dismay. "You're clowns!"

"They may be clowns, but they're not fools!"

Kroogie turned around to see who had spoken—it was a voice he didn't recognize, with a thick Russian accent. It came from Alexander, the calliope player who rarely spoke.

"Look pal," Kroogie said, "just who do you think you are?"

"Somebody who remembers history," Alexander replied. "You clowns want the same rewards as the exceptional performers like Atlas, even though you do not contribute in exceptional ways! This way of thinking is what destroyed my Russia."

"It was a terrifying failure," he added. "My family lived in poverty and struggled to escape, and now I see it start to happen in this circus."

He turned his attention to the twins. "You children must find Atlas," he said. "Tell him that if he comes back, we will make sure the ringmaster will reward him with everything he deserves."

Ethan shot a glance at the ringmaster, who clenched his fists in frustration. "I'll think about it," he said flatly.

The Tuttle family's search for Atlas began immediately. Mrs. Tuttle drove Ethan and Emily around town to put up the fliers they had created—sticking them on the windows of nearby businesses, light poles, and bus stops.

Mr. Tuttle took the photos of Atlas into the businesses to ask if the employees had seen him around town.

"Wait a minute," Ethan said. "Atlas isn't from around here, right? He was only in town for the circus."

"So maybe he's gone home?" Emily wondered.

"Nope, he's here," Mr. Tuttle replied as he exited the barber shop. "The barber saw Atlas yesterday, and I think I know where to find him," he added.

The Tuttle family's van pulled up to a gym on the edge of town. The twins began walking through the rows of treadmills and exercise machines inside.

"Over there!" Emily shouted, pointing to the weight room on the other end.

There they saw a large man sitting next to a much smaller one—it was Atlas, and Cannonball had found him too!

"Look who it is!" their little friend said, clapping his hands. "I found this guy just last night, eating at an all-you-can-eat buffet," he added with a chuckle.

"Yeah, I eat a lot!" he said, winking at the twins.

"Atlas, the circus is falling apart since you left," Ethan said.

"Serves them right," he replied. "Those guys need to stop pretending to be *victims*—people who have been hurt by someone else. They are only hurt because of their own choices to be lazy and jealous of others."

"But it does seem like you got special treatment which isn't fair to the others," Emily commented. "Doesn't that seem a little selfish?"

After pausing to think for a moment, the strongman lifted the twins onto his barbell. Mrs. Tuttle watched nervously as Atlas then began lifting the weights— and her children—into the air.

"Have you always been so strong?" Ethan asked as he and his sister rode up and down.

"Not at all," he replied. "In fact, I used to be a clown like you."

"Wait, what?" Emily shot back. "No way!"

"He's right," Cannonball said. "The last strongman, Hercules, was so impressed by Atlas's *work ethic*—his belief that hard work is a good thing—that he offered to train Atlas to be the new strongman before he retired."

"But Atlas was much skinnier back then!" Cannonball added, elbowing his big friend.

"I had to work harder than anybody else in the circus," Atlas explained. "I would wake up every morning so sore that I was unable to move," he added, flexing his thick arms. "And to get muscles like these you also have to eat a lot of special foods."

The twins realized that becoming a strongman was a lot harder than becoming a clown.

"All those years of hard work and sacrifice paid off," Cannonball said. "With Atlas as the star, the circus had never sold more tickets."

"The stuntmen, the acrobats, and the clowns also work hard," Emily said, looking at Atlas. "Why do you deserve more rewards than them?" she asked.

Atlas sat the twins on the bench to explain. "The value of anything is decided by two things: supply and demand. *Supply* is determined by how rare something is. If something is easy to come by, then people won't value it as much."

Atlas pulled out a bottle of water from his gym bag. "You wouldn't pay $20 for this, because there is an abundance of water here—it's not rare. There is a drinking fountain right over there for free! But what about in a desert where there's no supply of water?"

Ethan imagined being stranded in the Sahara Desert, his lips dry and cracking. "I would pay even more than $20 to get some water!" he said.

SUPPLY

Atlas smiled. "I would, too—and that's called *demand*. Demand is determined by how much people want something." He reached into his bag. "These kale chips were on sale today. Would you pay $20 for them?"

Emily squirmed. "You couldn't pay me $20 to eat those things," she said.

"That's probably why they're on sale," Cannonball joked. "Consumers wouldn't buy them at regular price. That tells the producer to lower the price or make a new product that people value more."

"My work was valued because it was in demand," Atlas said. "Things were good! But the clowns basically wanted *socialism*. They wanted equal rewards no matter what—or how much—they produced."

"Alexander talked about that," Emily replied. "He said the problems at the circus were just like what happened in Russia."

"That's the problem with socialism," Mr. Tuttle said. "If everybody gets the same rewards, how do you know what has value? Why would anyone work so hard to be a strongman if the reward was the same as becoming a clown, which isn't as hard? Socialism weakens the *incentive* to be better and work harder."

"If hard work wasn't rewarded, the circus would have lots of clowns and no strongmen," Cannonball added, making a funny face like a clown.

"Alexander was right," Mrs. Tuttle said.

# FAIR REWARDS

"Russia's government implemented socialism, and it didn't take long before everyone was consuming more than they produced. There was so little food that people had to wait in long lines just to get their equal amount of food to survive."

"That's why *personal responsibility* is so important," Atlas said. "Each of us should be free to enjoy the rewards of our labor, but also suffer the consequences if we are foolish or lazy. That's how to avoid the problems that happened in Russia— and that are happening now in the circus."

"Now you know why Atlas is the most valuable act—he's in short supply!" Cannonball said. "It's hard to find anyone stronger than him, he does the work of five men, and draws the biggest crowds."

"But the clowns don't understand supply and demand," Atlas added. "They demand rewards without supplying hard work. *That's* selfish!"

The twins hadn't considered that it was actually the clowns who were being selfish, rather than Atlas.

"I left because working around people who think they are victims was making me miserable," he said.

"What if we could get the ringmaster and the clowns to change their minds?" Ethan asked.

"It's worth a shot," Atlas replied. "But how?"

"Mrs. Tuttle and I will put out the word that you're returning," Mr. Tuttle said. "At tonight's show we'll pack every seat in the house—and show Kroogie and the ringmaster just how valuable you are."

Tickets were selling quickly that evening as people began streaming into the circus tent.

Mr. and Mrs. Tuttle came in and gave their kids a thumbs up to signal that their plan had worked.

Emily tried to hide her smile as the ringmaster scratched his head in confusion, wondering why so many people had shown up.

The large crowd made the performers excited, giving them energy to work hard to entertain the audience.

The clowns all did cartwheels around the elephant, who sprayed some water into the audience for fun. Only Alexander noticed her accidentally bumping into one of the tent poles.

"Watch out!" Alexander shouted, pointing to the pole. The construction crew didn't secure it well enough without Atlas—it was very heavy, after all. The giant tent looked like it might collapse on top of the audience.

Cannonball decided to improvise and quickly lit the fuse on his cannon, climbing inside. KABOOM! "Behold, the great Atlas!" he shouted as he flew through the air.

The famous strongman leaped from the audience, pushing Kroogie out of the path of the leaning pole, which he then grabbed. Atlas grunted and strained, slowly pushing it back into place.

The audience erupted in applause and cheers. They were happy to see the circus star return and impressed that he had stopped the pole from falling.

"Atlas saved your life!" Emily said, gently jabbing Kroogie in the ribs.

"It appears he also saved the circus..." the clown added, pointing to the packed seats.

The ringmaster stepped forward, shaking the strongman's hand. "I was wrong," he said, "and I'm sorry. I'll pay you what you deserve and you can keep your perks—you've earned them. Will you rejoin us?"

The strongman shot a glance at the twins who were giving him a big thumbs up.

"Sure, why not?" Atlas shrugged.

The End

"By the metaphysical nature of man and of existence, man has to maintain his life by his own effort; the values he needs—such as wealth or knowledge—are not given to him automatically, as a gift of nature, but have to be discovered and achieved by his own thinking and work."

—Ayn Rand

Using fiction to demonstrate the power of ideas, Ayn Rand's classic novel *Atlas Shrugged* portrays a society in which socialism attacks and alienates the innovators whose contributions are needed and without whom society begins to fall apart.

This book—read by millions—is especially helpful in visualizing the effects that laws have on people individually, and society more broadly.

With the power of a question ("Who is John Galt?") Rand helps the reader contemplate and understand the importance of allowing individuals to pursue their own interests and profit from their efforts. "Only a ghost can exist without material property," she writes. "Only a slave can work with no right to the product of his effort."

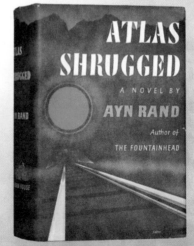

### The Author

Connor Boyack is president of Libertas Institute, a free market think tank in Utah. He is also president of The Association for Teaching Kids Economics, an organization that provides teachers with educational materials and lesson plans to teach economic ideas to their students in a fun and memorable way. Connor is the author of over a dozen books.

A California native and Brigham Young University graduate, Connor currently resides in Lehi, Utah, with his wife and two children.

### The Illustrator

Elijah Stanfield is owner of Red House Motion Imaging, a media production company in Washington.

A longtime student of Austrian economics, history, and the classical liberal philosophy, Elijah has dedicated much of his time and energy to promoting the ideas of free markets and individual liberty. Some of his more notable works include producing eight videos in support of Ron Paul's 2012 presidential candidacy. He currently resides in Richland, Washington, with his wife April and their six children.

Contact us at TuttleTwins.com!

# Glossary of Terms

**Consume:** To use a resource, such as a product or service.

**Demand:** The desire of consumers to obtain a product or service.

**Incentive:** A thing that motivates or encourages a person to do something.

**Personal Responsibility:** Embracing the consequences of your decisions and acting according to what you should be doing.

**Produce:** To create a resource such as a product or service.

**Socialism:** A political and economic system in which people are given products or services no matter what they produce.

**Supply:** The availability of a product or service to be consumed.

**Victim:** A person who has been hurt by someone else.

**Work Ethic:** A belief that hard work is virtuous and important.

# Discussion Questions

1. Was Atlas selfish?
2. Is anyone else entitled to the product of your labor?
3. What incentives exist that encourage you to work hard?
4. What do you produce?
5. Could the circus have survived without Atlas? Why or why not?
6. Why did the clowns act like victims?

## Don't Forget the Activity Workbook!

Visit **TuttleTwins.com/AtlasWorkbook** to download the PDF and provide your children with all sorts of activities to reinforce the lessons they learned in the book!